CW00958407

OUR SOLAR SYSTEM

Written by
Clare Oliver

Illustrated by

Jim Eldridge, Colin Howard and Stephen Sweet

p

This is a Parragon Book
This edition published in 2003

Parragon
Queen Street House
4 Queen Street
Bath BA1 1HE, UK

Copyright © Parragon 2001

Original book created by

David West ☂ Children's Books

All rights reserved. No part of this publication
may be reproduced, stored in a retrieval system, or
transmitted by any means, electronic, mechanical,
photocopying, recording or otherwise, without the
prior permission of the copyright holder.

British Library Cataloguing-in-Publication Data

A catalogue record for this book is available from
the British Library.

ISBN 1-40540-278-4

Printed in Dubai,U.A.E

Designers
Aarti Parmar
Rob Shone
Fiona Thorne
Illustrators
John Butler
Jim Eldridge
James Field
Andrew & Angela Harland
Colin Howard
Rob Jakeway
Mike Lacey
Sarah Lees
Gilly Marklew
Dud Moseley
Terry Riley
Sarah Smith
Stephen Sweet
Mike Taylor
Ross Watton
(SGA)
Ian Thompson
Cartoonist
Peter Wilks
(SGA)
Editor
James Pickering
Consultant
Steve Parker

CONTENTS

? What is the Solar System?

Solar means 'of the Sun'. The Solar System is centred around the Sun, the shining ball in the sky. It includes the family of nine planets orbiting (travelling around) the Sun, as well as the moons of these planets, and smaller objects, such as comets, asteroids, and bits of space rock. The powerful pull of an invisible force called gravity from the Sun stops these bodies from flying off into deepest space.

Saturn
Distance from Sun
1,427 million km
Diameter
129,660 km

Mars
Distance from Sun
228 million km
Diameter
6,796 km

Jupiter
Distance from Sun
778 million km
Diameter
142,984 km

Mercury
Distance from Sun
58 million km
Diameter
4,878 km

Earth
Distance from Sun
150 million km
Diameter
12,756 km

Venus
Distance from Sun
108 million km
Diameter
12,104 km

Uranus
Distance from Sun
2,870 million km
Diameter
51,118 km

Neptune
Distance from Sun
4,497 million km
Diameter
49,532 km

Pluto
Distance from Sun
5,900 million km
Diameter
2,360 km

Is it true?
All planets have one moon.

No. Our planet Earth has one moon, called the Moon. But many of the planets have more than one. Our neighbour Mars, for instance, has two! Only the two planets closest to the Sun – Mercury and Venus – have no moons at all.

Amazing! Saturn's not the only planet with rings. Saturn's rings are the easiest to see, but Jupiter, Neptune and Uranus have them, too. Saturn has seven main rings, and then hundreds of thinner rings, called ringlets.

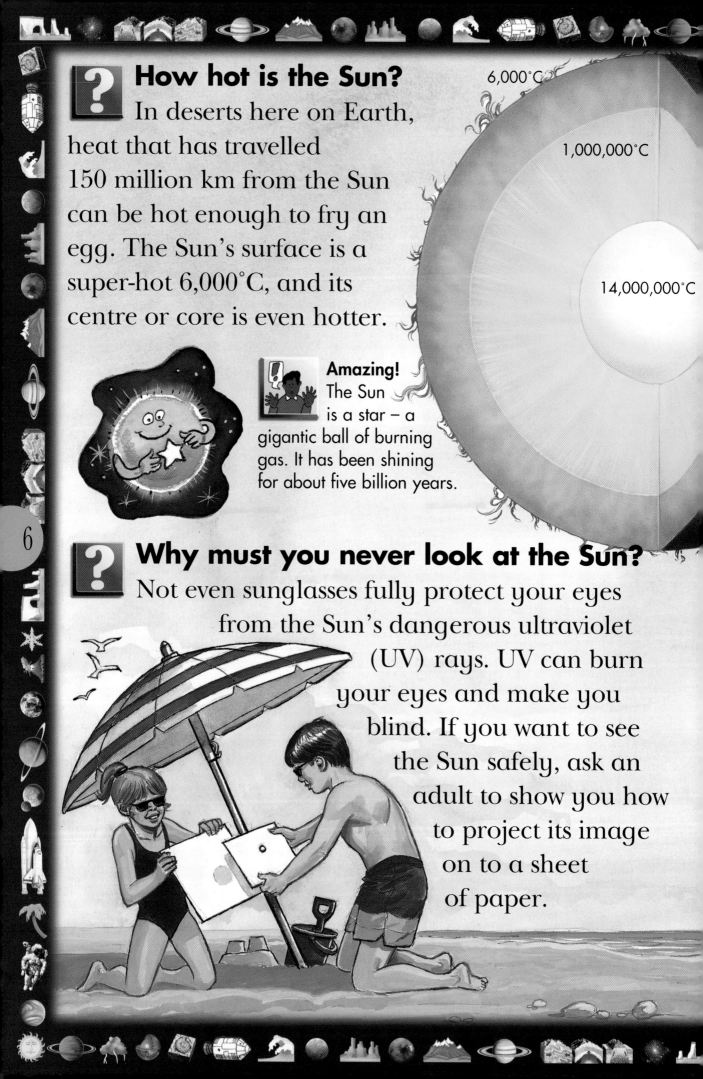

How hot is the Sun?

In deserts here on Earth, heat that has travelled 150 million km from the Sun can be hot enough to fry an egg. The Sun's surface is a super-hot 6,000°C, and its centre or core is even hotter.

6,000°C

1,000,000°C

14,000,000°C

Amazing!
The Sun is a star – a gigantic ball of burning gas. It has been shining for about five billion years.

Why must you never look at the Sun?

Not even sunglasses fully protect your eyes from the Sun's dangerous ultraviolet (UV) rays. UV can burn your eyes and make you blind. If you want to see the Sun safely, ask an adult to show you how to project its image on to a sheet of paper.

Is it true?
The Sun has spots.

Yes. The Sun is not the same colour all over. Some areas of its surface are darker. These spots are little pockets that are slightly cooler. Of course, sunspots are only 'little' compared to the Sun – some grow to be as large as Jupiter, the biggest planet in the Solar System!

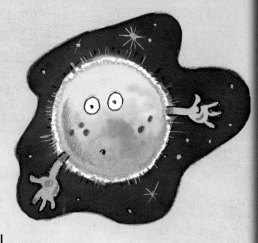

WARNING!
NEVER LOOK AT THE SUN, EVEN IF YOU'RE WEARING SUNGLASSES.

Total eclipse of the Sun

When does the Sun go out?

When there's a total eclipse. This happens when the Moon's path takes it between the Earth and the Sun, and the Moon casts a shadow across the surface of the Earth.

What does Mercury look like?

Planet Mercury looks very like our Moon. It's about the same size and it's covered in craters, where bits of space rock have crash-landed on its surface. The biggest crater is the Caloris Basin, which is about 1,300 km across. Mercury also has huge plains, rolling hills, deep gorges, chasms, and cliffs.

Earth

Mercury

Is it true?
Mercury is the smallest planet.

No. Mercury is only about a third the size of the Earth, but Pluto is even smaller. If you could put them on the scales, it would take 21 Plutos to balance one Mercury.

The surface of Mercury is covered with craters.

8

? Is Mercury the hottest planet?

Mercury is the planet closest to the Sun, but its neighbour Venus is even hotter, because it has clouds to keep in the heat.

The surface of Mercury is 350°C during the day, and minus 170°C at night.

? What is the weather like on Mercury?

Mercury doesn't have any weather, because it has no air and hardly any atmosphere. That means there are no clouds to shield the surface of the planet from the baking-hot Sun during the day, or to keep in the heat at night. There is no wind or rain on Mercury, either.

 Amazing!.Mercury is the fastest planet. Mercury zooms around the Sun in just 88 days, at an incredible 173,000 kph. That makes it faster than any space rocket ever invented.

The planet Venus seen close to the Moon

? When is a star not a star?

When it's a planet! Venus is sometimes called the 'evening star' because it's so bright it's one of the first points of light we see shining as it gets dark. Planets don't make their own light – they reflect the Sun's light.

Is it true?
Venus is bigger than the Earth.

No. Venus is a fraction smaller than the Earth, but not by much. Venus is about 12,104 km across, whereas Earth is about 650 km wider. Venus's mass is about four-fifths of Earth's.

Earth

Venus

Amazing!
Venus is named after a goddess. Venus was the name of the Roman goddess of love and beauty – just right for the planet, which many people think is the most beautiful object in the sky.

? How can a day be longer than a year?

A day is the amount of time a planet takes to spin on its axis, and a year is the time it takes to travel around the Sun. Venus spins on its axis very slowly, but orbits the Sun more quickly than Earth. A day on Venus lasts 243 Earth-days, but a year is only 225 Earth-days.

Volcanic eruption on Venus

? What's special about our planet?

As far as we know, Earth is the only planet in the Solar System that has life.

As well as warmth from the Sun, the other main ingredient for life is liquid water. Earth has plenty of water – in total, it covers about three-quarters of the planet's surface!

Is it true?
There was life on Earth from the start.

No. When Earth first formed it was extremely hot and there was no oxygen. Over millions of years, the planet cooled, oceans formed and oxygen was made. The first life on Earth appeared about 3 billion years ago.

Earth seen from space

What does Earth look like from space?

It looks beautiful – blue with swirling white clouds. Astronauts in space spend most of their free time gazing at it. They can even make out cities, when they are lit up at night with twinkling lights.

Amazing! The Earth is magnetic. At the centre of the Earth is a core of a molten metal called iron, which makes our planet like a giant magnet. This is what pulls the needle on a compass towards the magnetic North Pole.

Why does our sky go dark at night?

Like all planets, the Earth is spinning as it orbits the Sun. When your part of the planet is facing away from the Sun, its light is blocked out. At the same time, it is daytime for people on the opposite side of the Earth.

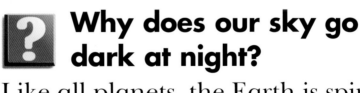

Why does the Moon have so many craters?

Because it has been pelted by so many space rocks and has no atmosphere to protect it. One of the biggest craters, called Bailly, is nearly 300 km across. You can make out some of the craters using a good pair of binoculars.

Meteorite hitting the Moon

New Moon

Crescent Moon

First quarter Moon

Gibbous Moon

Why does the Moon change shape?

It doesn't really – it's ball-shaped just like the Earth, but as the Moon travels around the Earth, you see different amounts of its sunlit half. It seems to change gradually from a crescent to a disc, and back again.

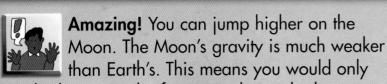

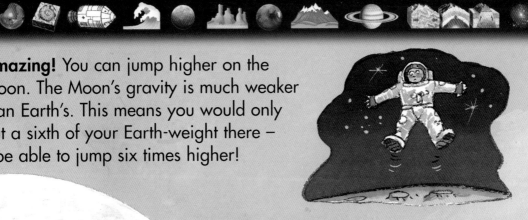

Amazing! You can jump higher on the Moon. The Moon's gravity is much weaker than Earth's. This means you would only weigh about a sixth of your Earth-weight there – and you'd be able to jump six times higher!

Full Moon

? What is the dark side of the Moon?

It's the part of the Moon that we can never see from Earth. The Moon takes the same time to orbit the Earth as it does to spin once. This means the same side of the Moon always faces away from the Earth.

15

 Is it true?
There are seas on the Moon.

Yes and no. There are dark, rocky plains and craters called maria (Latin for 'seas'), but they don't contain water. The first astronauts to visit the Moon landed on the Sea of Tranquillity.

Earth

Mars

? Which is the red planet?

Mars was named after the Roman god of war, because of its blood-red colour. The planet looks rusty red because its surface is covered with iron-rich soil and rock. There are no seas on Mars, and it is very cold.

? Does Mars have ice at its poles?

Yes. Its south pole is mostly 'dry ice', which is frozen carbon dioxide gas. At the north pole there may be frozen water, mixed with the frozen carbon dioxide. There may be frozen water underground on Mars, too.

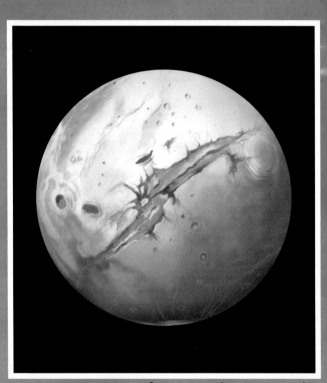

One of Mars's polar caps, at the bottom of the planet

Is it true?
There is life on Mars.

No. Or at least, there's no sure sign of any. But long ago, Mars had flowing rivers of water, so there could have been life once, and there may be fossils buried underground.

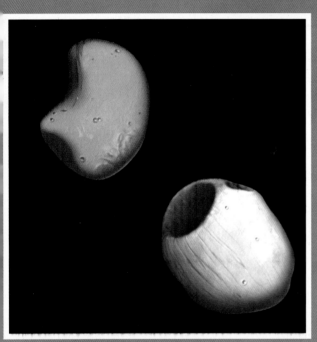

Phobos
(about 15 km long)

Deimos
(about 27 km long)

? What are Mars's moons like?

Mars's two tiny moons, Deimos and Phobos, are not round like our Moon. They look more like baked potatoes! They might have been asteroids (space rocks) that Mars captured with its gravity.

Amazing! There's a record-breaking volcano on Mars. Olympus Mons is about 600 km across and towers over 25 km high. It's the Solar System's biggest volcano. Long ago it spurted out runny rivers of black lava.

The Martian surface, showing Olympus Mons

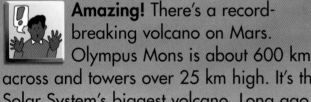

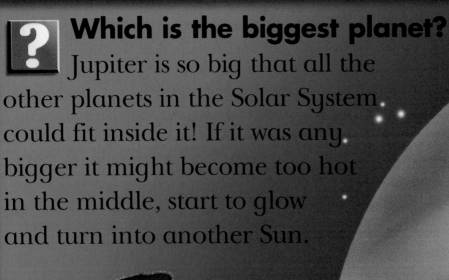

? Which is the biggest planet?

Jupiter is so big that all the other planets in the Solar System could fit inside it! If it was any bigger it might become too hot in the middle, start to glow and turn into another Sun.

Is it true?
Jupiter's stripy.

Yes. The planet looks like it's wearing a giant pair of pyjamas, because of its bands of cloud. They're made of frozen crystals of water, ammonia and other chemicals.

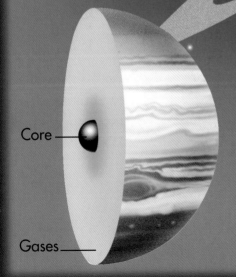

Core

Gases

? What is Jupiter made of?

Jupiter is one of the planets known as the gas giants. About 90 per cent of it is made of gases called hydrogen and helium. At the centre of Jupiter is a small, rocky core, about as big as the Earth.

Amazing! You could fit two Earths inside the Great Red Spot, which is about 40,000 km across.

Jupiter

Earth

Where is the storm that never stops?

Violent winds whip up storms all over the planet Jupiter, but the Great Red Spot is the largest. It has been raging away for over 300 years!

The Great Red Spot is a giant storm on Jupiter.

Looking at Jupiter from Io

Which world has most volcanoes?

Jupiter's closest moon, Io, is orange and yellow, because of the sulphur from all its active volcanoes. If you could survive the intense heat, you'd realise that Io smells of rotten eggs!

Which moon is bigger than a planet?

Jupiter's moon Ganymede is the largest moon in the Solar System. At 5,276 km across, it is bigger than Mercury! Another of Jupiter's moons, Callisto, is a similar size to Mercury.

Ganymede

Looking at Jupiter from Ganymede

20

Io

Europa

Which moon might have life?

Jupiter's moon Europa is covered by a thick crust of ice. The ice looks smooth, like frozen water, but it also has lots of cracks. Scientists think there is a liquid ocean beneath the ice – and where there's water, there might be life!

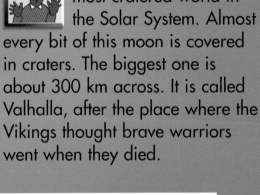

Amazing! Callisto is the most cratered world in the Solar System. Almost every bit of this moon is covered in craters. The biggest one is about 300 km across. It is called Valhalla, after the place where the Vikings thought brave warriors went when they died.

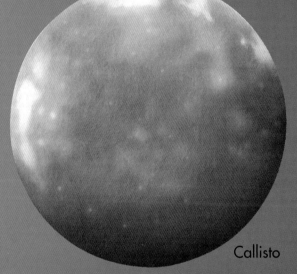

Callisto

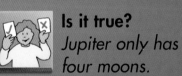

Is it true?
Jupiter only has four moons.

No. Galileo discovered the four biggest – Callisto, Ganymede, Europa and Io – in 1610. Since then, astronomers have discovered 13 smaller moons as well, making a total of 17.

Saturn's rings viewed from its upper atmosphere

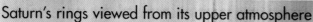 Are Saturn's rings solid?

No – they look solid, but they are made up of millions of chunks of ice and rock. The smallest chunks are about the size of a golf ball, while the biggest are about a kilometre wide.

 Amazing! You could fit about 740 Earths into Saturn. It is the Solar System's second largest planet, after Jupiter. Its rings are 270,000 km across – about twice the width of the planet.

Saturn

Earth

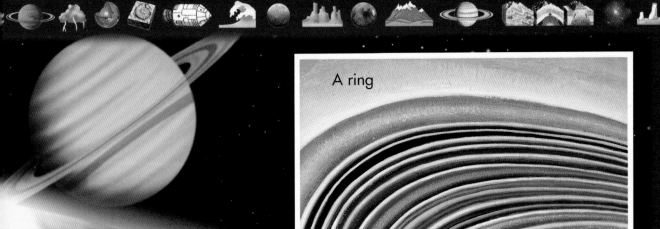

A ring

B ring

C ring

Saturn viewed
from above Titan

? How many moons does Saturn have?

Saturn has at least 18 moons, but there may be more. The biggest is Titan – the second largest moon in the Solar System. Titan is covered by clouds, so we can't see its surface.

? Do Saturn's rings have names?

Not really, but scientists have given each ring a letter so that they know which one they are talking about. There are seven main rings, of which the three brightest are A, B and C.

23

Is it true?
Saturn is light enough to float.

Yes. Saturn is made up of liquid and gas, with a small rocky centre. It is so light that, if there was an ocean big enough, the planet would float on it like a boat!

William Herschel

Uranus was discovered in 1781. The man who found it, William Herschel, was not expecting to find a planet at all. He thought he was pointing his homemade telescope at a distant star.

? **How many moons does Uranus have?**

Uranus has at least 17 moons – but there could be more to discover. They are all named after characters from English literature. The main ones are Oberon, Titania, Umbriel, Ariel and Miranda. Ophelia and Cordelia are the closest.

24

Amazing! The poles on Uranus are warmer than the equator. Because Uranus is tilted on its side, the poles are the warmest places on the planet. Summer at the south pole lasts 42 years!

Approaching Uranus through its rings

Miranda

Uranus

Earth

? Why is Uranus blue?

The bluish-green is the colour of methane, a stinky gas that makes up part of Uranus's atmosphere. The other gases in the air there are hydrogen and helium – the gas we use to fill party balloons.

25

Is it true?
Uranus was nearly called George.

Yes. When Herschel discovered the new planet, he wanted to name it after the English king at the time, George III. In the end, it was called Uranus, after the Greek god of the sky.

George

? Which planet has pulling power?

Astronomers knew Neptune must be there before they saw it! They could tell something big was pulling Uranus and they were able to predict exactly where Neptune was – almost 4.5 billion kilometres away from the Sun.

Storm on Neptune

? What's the weather like on Neptune?

Very, very windy! Winds rip across the planet all the time, much faster than any winds on Earth. There are also lots of storms on Neptune, which show up as dark spots. This means Neptune's appearance is constantly changing.

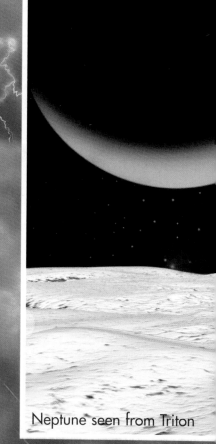

Neptune seen from Triton

Is it true?
Triton is Neptune's only moon.

No. Neptune has seven other moons, but Triton and Nereid are the main ones. Triton is the biggest. It is 2,706 km across – about four-fifths the size of our Moon.

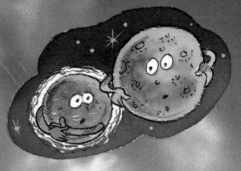

Where would you find pink snow?

When the gas nitrogen freezes, it looks like pink snow! There is frozen nitrogen at Neptune's north and south poles, and at the poles of its largest moon, Triton. So far from the Sun, Neptune and its moons are bitterly cold places.

Amazing! Triton is one of the coldest places ever recorded! The temperature on the ice-covered moon is minus 236° C. That's just 37°C from being the lowest possible temperature in the entire Universe!

Neptune's windy surface

27

Pluto's icy surface is minus 220°C

? Which is the coldest planet?

Pluto is the coldest planet of all, which is not surprising, because it is usually the farthest from the Sun. Inside, it is made up of ice and rock, and the planet has a thick layer of ice over the top.

Is it true?
Pluto was named after a cartoon dog.

No. Pluto was the name of the Greek god of the underworld. Also, the first two letters of Pluto, 'P' and 'L' are the initials of Percival Lowell, who first predicted a planet beyond Neptune.

? Who found Pluto's moon?

An American called Jim Christy discovered Pluto's moon in 1978. He called it Charon, which was his wife's name, and also the name of the man who ferried people to the underworld in Ancient Greek mythology.

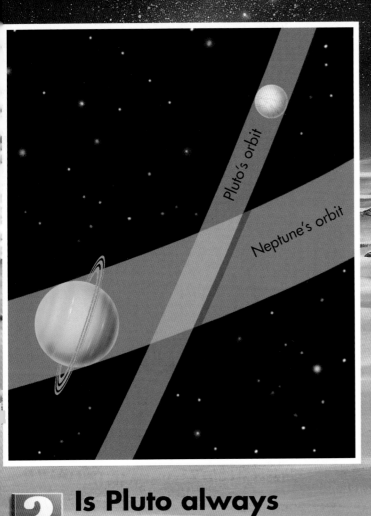

Amazing! Pluto is smaller than a country. Pluto is a tiny planet – the smallest in the Solar System. At 2,360 km across, it is smaller than the United States or Russia!

? Is Pluto always farthest from the Sun?

Pluto is so far away from the Sun that it takes 248 years just to orbit it once! But Pluto's orbit is a funny shape. For 20 years of its orbit, Pluto dips in closer to the Sun than Neptune. When this happens, Neptune is the farthest planet in the Solar System.

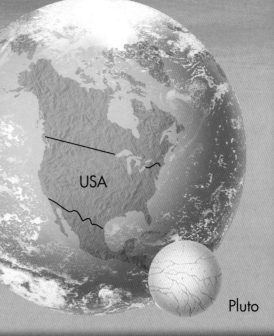

USA

Pluto

Asteroids orbiting the Sun

? Are there any other planets?

There are lots of minor planets, known as asteroids, in our Solar System. About 3,500 of these lumps of space rock are orbiting the Sun.

Comet with its glowing tail

? Are there snowballs in space?

Yes – comets are balls of ice and rock. They go whizzing through the Solar System leaving behind a glowing tail of gas. As a comet gets closer to the Sun, it gets hotter and its tail becomes longer. Some comets even grow a second tail. In the past, the arrival of a comet was thought to be a magical event.

Shooting stars

Amazing! We can tell when comets will come back. Some comets follow a regular course, so we know exactly when we'll next see them. Halley's Comet will next fly past the Earth in 2061.

Is it true?
Asteroids weigh the same as the Earth.

No. Even if all of the asteroids in the Solar System were lumped together, the Earth would still weigh more than a thousand times as much.

? What is a shooting star?

A shooting star, or meteor, happens when a tiny space rock, called a meteoroid, enters Earth's atmosphere and burns up. We see it as a streak of light across the sky. Meteor showers happen when our planet passes through a group of meteoroids.

Glossary

Asteroid A small rocky body which orbits the Sun.

Atmosphere The gases or air surrounding a planet.

Axis The imaginary line around which a planet spins.

Comet A body of ice and rock with a long glowing tail that orbits the Sun.

Eclipse When light from the Sun or Moon is blocked out. A solar eclipse is when the Moon passes between the Earth and Sun, casting a shadow on the Earth. A lunar eclipse is when Earth passes between the Moon and Sun.

Fossil The remains of an ancient animal or plant preserved in rock.

Gravity The force of attraction between two objects.

Meteoroid A small lump of space rock.

Moon An object in space orbiting a planet.

Orbit To travel around.

Planet A body of gas or rock orbiting a star. Planets are not heavy enough to be stars. They shine because they reflect the light of the star they are orbiting.

Poles The points at either end of a planet's axis, known as the north and south poles.

Solar System Our Sun and everything that travels around it.

Star A huge ball of super-hot burning gas.

32

Index